13 The ALAMO Book of Days

Published by Native Sun Productions
Carolyn Raine-Foreman, Editor
P. O. Box 2075
Valparaiso, IN 46384
www.nativesunproductions.com

13 The Alamo Book of Days
www.alamo13days.com

Author – Glenn Effler
Photography – Gary L. Foreman
Illustrations – Mark Lemon
Cover Design – William Hamilton and Lynn Beda
Photo Editing – Michael Jr. and Susan Gamble, Gamble Graphics
Book Design – Lynn Beda, Beda Design
Printer – Modern Litho-Print Co.

First Printing March 2011
ISBN-10: 0-9740676-2-8
ISBN-13: 978-0-9740676-2-9
Manufactured in the United States of America

TABLE OF CONTENTS

Introduction

Epilogue

About the Authors

Acknowledgments

INTRODUCTION

December, 1835. It was a miracle…or so it seemed. The volunteer Texian army notched another stunning victory over a numerically superior Mexican army. The most recent triumph came at the expense of General Martin Perfecto de Cós, commander of the Mexican forces occupying San Antonio de Béxar, a Texas city on the west bank of the slow moving San Antonio River. The battle for Béxar was fought street-to-street, house-to-house, and hand-to-hand. After 3 days of brutal fighting, the Mexican soldados defending the town capitulated, vowing never to take up arms against the 1824 Constitution. General Cós and his defeated troops marched south toward the Rio Grande.

Now that Béxar was back in Texian hands and the vanquished Mexican army was returning to Mexico, the question on everybody's mind was, "is the war over?" Some in the army believed the hostilities had ended - at least until spring - and returned to their homes to care and provide for their families. But hundreds of others, mostly volunteers from the United States, had nowhere to go. These restless and adventurous men stripped the town clean of food, clothing, medicine, draft animals and other valuable military supplies, headed toward Matamoros, Mexico but ended up in the fortified mission at Goliad 90 miles to the southeast.

By January of 1836, the break-up of the Texian army left about 80 volunteers to garrison San Antonio under the command of Colonel James Neill. Colonel Neill was given the daunting task of fortifying the Alamo, an old Spanish mission that was more like a land-locked Spanish galleon due to the 18 or so cannon that guarded its thick walls. Desperate for money, supplies, and most importantly, men, Neill petitioned the acting governor for immediate aid. The resource-strapped Texas government would send what it could. In the mean time, General Sam Houston dispatched frontier legend James Bowie and 30 men to Béxar to reinforce the depleted garrison. Houston believed the position was untenable and had plans to destroy the town's fortifications; the Alamo too if the governor approved. However, Bowie and Colonel Neill had other ideas. The 2 Texian leaders were convinced San Antonio was too important to abandon and decided that they'd "rather die in these ditches" then surrender the town to the Mexican army that was rumored to be heading

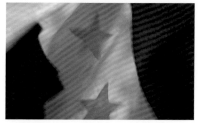

their way. They began to prepare the Alamo for eventual battle and went about transforming this former place of worship into a makeshift fortress.

On February 3rd, Lieutenant Colonel William Barret Travis entered Béxar with nearly 30 men. The 26 year old Alabama lawyer cut quite a figure. He was tall, handsome, with auburn hair and eyes that were fiery and intense. He was a passionate orator, an absolute romantic, a voracious reader of Sir Walter Scott and Lord Byron and guided by the tenets of duty, honor, country. A skilled rider, he envisioned himself at the head of legions of finely mounted horsemen and leading them in a desperate battle against an evil foe. Instead, he found himself commanding a small unit of the newly formed Texian cavalry. Garrison duty was not where he saw himself and Béxar wasn't where he wanted to be. However, like a good soldier he obediently but reluctantly accepted his assignment. Doubtful of his situation at first, he soon recognized San Antonio as a valuable frontier post and quickly sided with Neill and Bowie. In a letter to the governor he wrote: "We consider death preferable to disgrace, which would be the result of giving up a Post which has been so dearly won." The acting Texas government agreed, "We cannot be driven from the post of Honor and the sacred cause of freedom." San Antonio de Béxar must not fall into the hands of the enemy.

Colonel Neill received word of an illness in his family and decided to take a 10-day furlough to attend to matters. The garrison and the Alamo were shaping-up well and Neill felt the men would be fine until he returned. Besides, the Mexican army, rumored to be led by General Santa Anna himself, was not expected to threaten Béxar for at least another 2 to 3 weeks.

Prior to his departure, Colonel Neill appointed Travis as acting commander of the garrison. Neill probably preferred that Bowie command in his absence but Travis was an officer in the regular army and Bowie was a volunteer. Neill's hands were tied. 40 year old Jim Bowie was incensed, as were his men. He protested, got roaring drunk, and made a spectacle of himself. However, the following day a somewhat contrite Bowie acknowledged the need for unity and suggested Travis and himself share command of the Alamo garrison. Bowie would be responsible for the volunteers and Travis the army regulars. The 2 leaders came to an accord and peace was momentarily restored.

Shortly after William Travis arrived in Béxar, another prominent figure appeared in town to lend a hand. He was a former United States Congressman, an experienced Indian fighter, a prodigious bear hunter, and known for his prowess with a long gun and humorous story telling. He was the celebrated Tennessean, David Crockett. At nearly 50 years of age he was a living legend who could still "whip his weight in wildcats." He rode into the Alamo along with 15 other volunteers to aid the Texians in their "noble cause." The stage was now set. All but one cast member was in San Antonio and he was well on his way and closer than anyone believed.

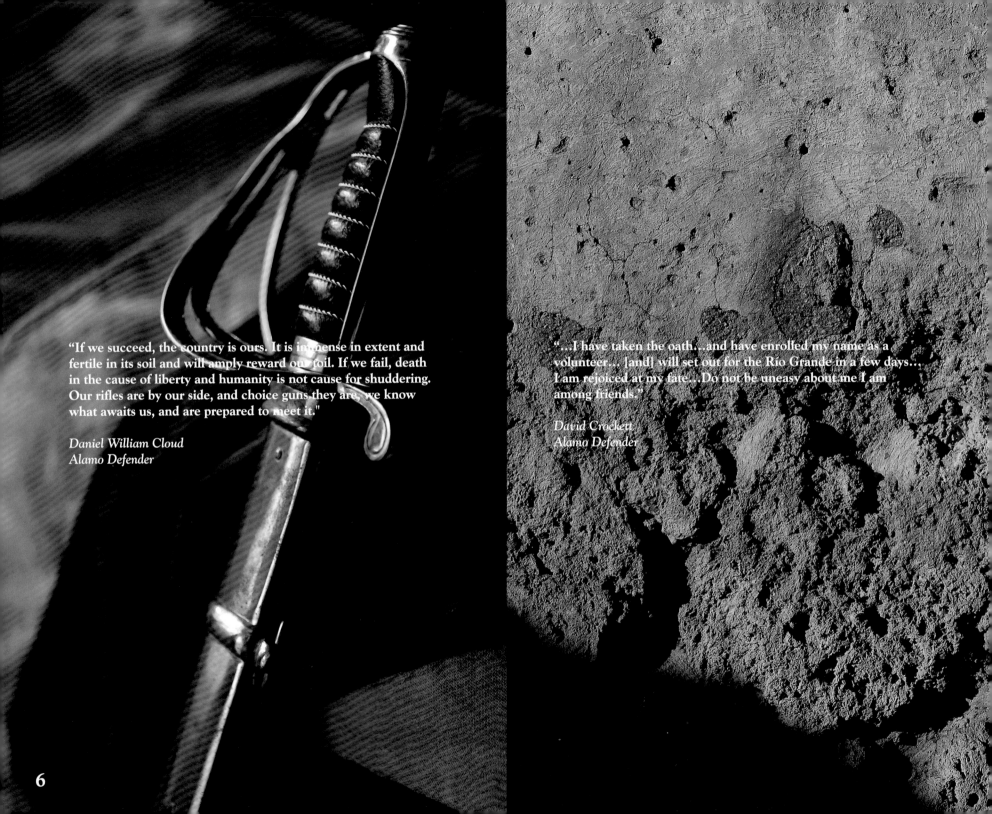

"If we succeed, the country is ours. It is immense in extent and fertile in its soil and will amply reward our toil. If we fail, death in the cause of liberty and humanity is not cause for shuddering. Our rifles are by our side, and choice guns they are, we know what awaits us, and are prepared to meet it."

Daniel William Cloud
Alamo Defender

"...I have taken the oath...and have enrolled my name as a volunteer... [and] will set out for the Rio Grande in a few days... I am rejoiced at my fate...Do not be uneasy about me I am among friends."

David Crockett
Alamo Defender

"Take care of my little boy. If the country should be saved, I may make him a splendid fortune; but if the country should be lost, and I should perish, he will have nothing but the proud recollection that he is the son of the man who died for his country."

William B. Travis
Alamo Defender

They were the aggressors, we the attacked, they the ingrates, we the benefactors. When they were in want we had given them sustenance, yet as soon as they gained strength they used it to destroy us.

Lt. Col. Jose Enrique de la Peña

7

Texian Order of Battle

Colonel James Bowie

Lieutenant Colonel William B Travis

Blazeby's Infantry Company

Baker's Infantry Company

Carey's Artillery Company

Forsyth's Cavalry Company

Seguín's Cavalry Company

Harrison's Company of Tennessee Mounted Volunteers

18-21 cannon of varying caliber.

Mexican Order of Battle

Commander: General of Brigade Joaquín Ramírez y Sesma

Deputy Commander: Colonel Eulogio González

Jimenez Permanent Battalion

Matamoros Permanent Battalion

Dolores Permanent Regiment

Artillery Company

Two each 8, 6 and 4 pound cannon with two 7-inch howitzers

8

Day 1 Tuesday, February 23

"The Enemy Are in View"

The past evening's fandango, an all out celebration honoring the birthday of revered U.S. President George Washington, had finally concluded just before sunrise. The huge festivity that began in the streets of Béxar ended in the local cantinas after a sudden rain storm sent the partiers indoors. The men of the Alamo garrison, now 150 strong, lay about sleeping or struggling with a hangover. The day started quietly enough but the dawn's silence soon gave way to a crescendo of noise emanating from the muddy streets. The Béxareños were leaving.

Creaking cart wheels accompanied by groaning oxen and the raucous braying of burros replaced the quiet stillness of the morning air. Small children sat atop overloaded baskets while older ones held onto their mother's skirt as they gave doe-eyed looks to the Texians they were leaving behind. The clatter and squealing of ox carts and the anxious, in-discernible voices of townsfolk woke the sleeping Texians that morning. The bleary-eyed men peered out windows or doors trying to make sense of the unexpected and strident exodus in the streets. And the morning's peculiar activities did not go unnoticed by the garrison's newly appointed commander, Colonel Travis, who watched with a mounting sense of uneasiness.

The growing number of Béxareños filing out of town caused Travis serious concern. Some of the nervous townsfolk were brought before the garrison commander and asked about the sudden goings-on. The responses were generally the same, "We're going out to prepare the fields for spring planting," but Travis wasn't persuaded by their answers and he continued to probe for the truth. He didn't have to wait long. An unknown local, possibly a Tejano (a native born Texan of Mexican heritage), brought word to Travis that a messenger had arrived the night before, warning all Béxareños to evacuate the town by dawn; Santa Anna's army was just 8 miles away at Leon Creek.

San Fernando Cathedral, Main Plaza, San Antonio de Bexar in 1836 (Image by Jim Boddie)

Scouts Sutherland and Smith reconnoiter west of Béxar and come upon the vanguard of Santa Anna's Army of Expedition.

Having learned the Mexican army might be close, Travis placed a lookout in the single tower of San Fernando Church on Main Plaza with orders to ring the bell if he sees enemy movement. Around noon, the excited sentinel rang the church bell wildly and pointed to the west. "The enemy are in view." Still not trusting this confirmation of activity, Travis dispatched 2 riders, John Sutherland and John Smith, toward the west. If the 2 scouts returned at anything other than a walk, the sentry was to ring the church's bell to signal the Texians to retreat into the Alamo.

As the riders topped the Alazan Heights a mile and a half west of town, they saw 1,500 soldados of the Vanguard Brigade, 1st Division, Army of the North commanded by General of Brigade Joaquín Ramírez y Sesma. Both men spurred their horses around, but the muddy road caused Sutherland's horse to fall, breaking his gun and pinning him underneath his animal. Sutherland got up slowly; his leg was badly wrenched. Smith assisted him in remounting and the 2 galloped back into San Antonio.

Chaos followed the bell. Travis began to shout orders and give direction. The garrison that had been lying about all morning was suddenly moving with energy and purpose. Men grabbed their guns, food, personal belongings or whatever they could carry. Jim Bowie and a few others were seen herding cattle into the former mission as vaqueros had done nearly a century before. During the withdrawal, 90 bushels of corn were discovered in abandoned jacales (crude huts) just south of the Alamo and swiftly carried inside. But not everyone was in a hurry to evacuate the town. Some men (possibly Tejanos) remained in Military Plaza long enough to allow the approaching army to see them raise and then lower the Mexican tri-color flag with 2 stars, replacing the eagle, snake and cactus, signifying Texas and Coahuila as 2 separate states in the Mexican Republic.

Mexican Soldado with cowhide knapsack (recreation)

Texas and Coahuila Flag
The Mexicans saw this flag raised in defiance in Main Plaza before taking the town on Feb. 23.

Texian Scout calls out alarm (recreation)

With shouts of "Viva Santa Anna!" and "Viva El Presidente!" the infantry marches by Santa Anna and his staff atop the Alazan Heights.

11

David Crockett 1786-1836

The Texians, some with families, moved anxiously west along Portrero Street toward the footbridge that crossed the San Antonio River. Artillery Captain Almaron Dickinson rode up to the house where his wife Susanna and their baby daughter had been staying and shouted: "The Mexicans are upon us. Give me the babe and jump up behind me." Dickinson took the young child in his arms while Susanna climbed on back. The anxious trio galloped across the river ford and through the south gate to safety. While most of the men were racing to the Alamo on foot, David Crockett and John Sutherland also rode their horses across the shallow ford below the bridge. They trotted into the fort and went looking for Travis. Inside the Alamo, men were scrambling with last minute preparations, wrestling cannon into position, or loading their muskets. Much of the garrison began to crowd the south and west walls of the mission's large compound trying to catch a glimpse of the Mexican army as it entered the town.

In his headquarters along the west wall, Travis wasted no time and hastily penned a missive to the mayor of Gonzales, a small settlement 70 miles to the east: "The enemy in large force is in sight. We want men and provisions. Send them to us. We have 150 men and are determined to defend the Alamo to the last. Give us assistance".

Travis handed the message to a courier who galloped out the east gate and toward the Gonzales Road. Minutes later, Crockett and Sutherland rode up to the fort's headquarters and reported to Travis. Hobbled, in pain, but still willing to do his duty, John Sutherland would ride to Gonzales and beyond to spread the news and raise volunteers. David Crockett approached Travis seeking direction. "Colonel, here am I. Assign me to a position, and I and my boys will try to defend it." Travis knew just the place for the reputed "Lion of the West." He would entrust Crockett and his "boys" with protecting the 8-foot high palisade wall that stretched 116 feet from the church to the south wall. Although it appeared the fort's weakest point, it was supported by a 4-pounder cannon and an outer barrier of felled trees making it a rather formidable position.

East side of the Alamo (from The Illustrated Alamo:1836)

"Colonel, here am I. Assign me a position, and I and my boys will try to defend it." (David Crockett)

When the defenders were safely within the Alamo, the cazadores (light infantrymen/riflemen) entered Main Plaza and immediately raised a red banner from the San Fernando's tower. There was no mistaking the message. By hoisting the blood-red flag, the Mexicans were signaling the men of the Alamo that no quarter would be given…no prisoners. An indignant Colonel Travis responded to the harsh threat with his own style of bravado. From the southwest corner of the Alamo he gave order for the fort's largest and most lethal cannon, the 18-pounder, to fire a round in reply to the flag of death flapping in the wind. The Mexicans returned this fire from howitzers assembled in an artillery park off the town's Main Plaza. The shells landed inside the compound but did no harm or damage.

Laying prostrate on a cot and feeling ill, a pale Jim Bowie called to his friends, Juan Seguín and fort engineer Green B. Jameson and asked about the exchange of cannon fire. Bowie was concerned young Travis may have acted too rashly in his response to the red flag. He had Seguín scribble a hasty note in Spanish, inquiring about a possible parley. He handed the message to Jameson who then rode out of the Alamo under a white flag of truce. Meeting Jameson on the small footbridge was Mexican Chief of Staff, Colonel Juan N. Almonte. Jameson asked Santa Anna's English-speaking aid if honorable terms would be tendered if the garrison was to surrender. Almonte said he would pass the letter on to his General and the impromptu meeting ended.

Travis watched the act on the bridge as it played out. He was angered by what he saw. It was agreed that he and Bowie would operate in concert and sign all correspondence jointly but Bowie violated the terms by acting independently. Travis would have his say.

Captain Albert Martin, a Rhode Islander, carried Travis' message to the bridge, and like Jameson, met with Colonel Almonte. This time, Almonte delivered Santa Anna's terms to the inquiring rebel commanders. The men in the Alamo must surrender without condition or face the inevitable consequences. Once again, both Travis and Bowie found common ground. The monstrous 18-pounder shook the countryside as it sent another round of defiance at the Mexican army. The Siege of the Alamo had officially begun.

Mission Concepcion –
2 miles south of the Alamo

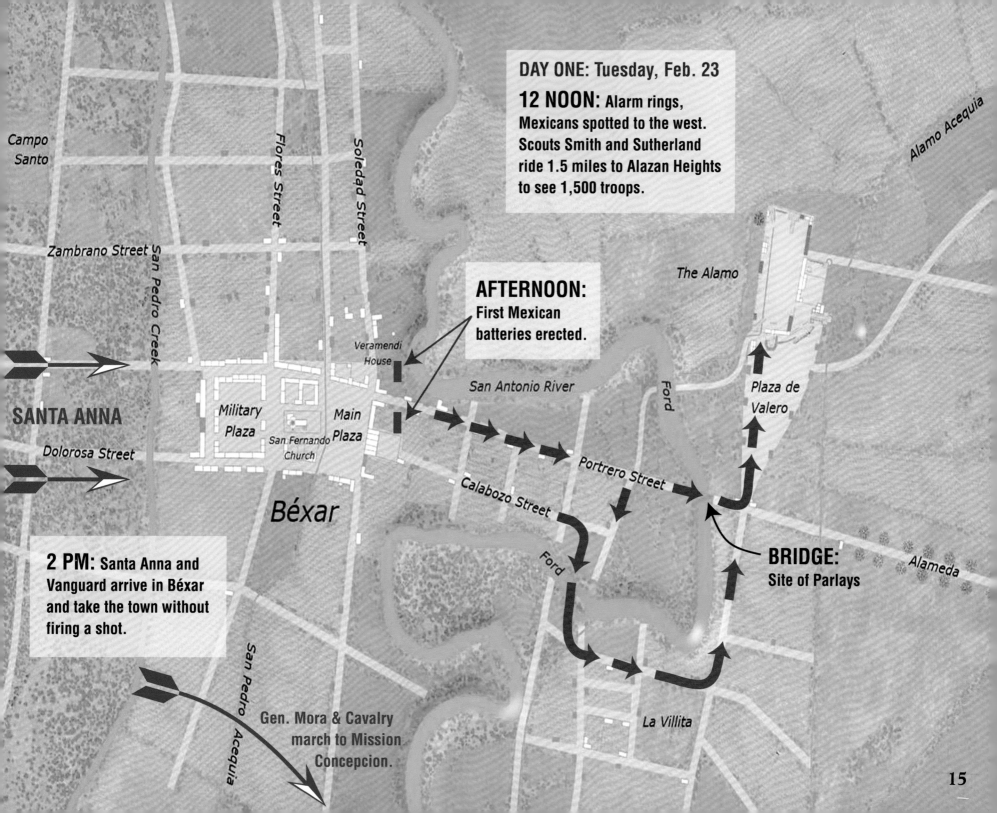

DAY ONE: Tuesday, Feb. 23

12 NOON: Alarm rings, Mexicans spotted to the west. Scouts Smith and Sutherland ride 1.5 miles to Alazan Heights to see 1,500 troops.

AFTERNOON:
First Mexican batteries erected.

The Alamo

Alamo Acequia

Campo Santo

Zambrano Street

Flores Street

Soledad Street

San Pedro Creek

SANTA ANNA

Dolorosa Street

Military Plaza

San Fernando Church

Main Plaza

Veramendi House

San Antonio River

Plaza de Valero

Ford

Béxar

Calabozo Street

Portrero Street

Ford

BRIDGE:
Site of Parlays

Alameda

2 PM: Santa Anna and Vanguard arrive in Béxar and take the town without firing a shot.

San Pedro Acequia

Gen. Mora & Cavalry march to Mission Concepcion.

La Villita

All great nations have their creation prose.
Inspiring documents like the United States Declaration of Independence,
the Preamble to the US Constitution, etc, were composed by men
who understood the power of words. In Texas that duty fell to Travis.
His memory is preserved for his command of the Alamo
but also for the creation of the letter.

Commandancy of the Alamo—
Bejar Fby. 24th 1836
To the People of Texas & all Americans in the world—
Fellow citizens & compatriots—
I am besieged, by a thousand or more of the Mexicans under
Santa Anna—I have sustained a continual Bombardment &
cannonade for 24 hours & have not lost a man—The enemy
has demanded a Surrender at discretion, otherwise, the garrison
are to be put to the sword, if the fort is taken—I have answered
the demand with a cannon shot, & our flag still waves
proudly from the wall—I shall never Surrender or retreat
Then, I can on you in the name of Liberty, of patriotism &
every thing dear to the American character, to come to our aid,
with all dispatch—The enemy is receiving reinforcements daily &
will no doubt increase to three or four thousand in four or five days.
If this call is neglected, I am determined to sustain myself as long as
possible & die like a soldier who never forgets what is due to
his own honor & that of his country
Victory or Death

William Barret Travis
Lt. Col. Comdt

P. S. The lord is on our side
When the enemy appears in sight we had not three bushels of corn—
We have since found in deserted houses 80 or 90 bushels & got into
the walls 20 or 30 head of Beeves—
Travis

Day 2 Wednesday February 24

"To the People of Texas"

Jim Bowie awoke on the morning of the 24th with a high fever and his deep wracking cough had become much worse. He tried to raise himself up but it was no good. He slumped back down in his cot and sent for Travis and Crockett. Bowie had finally met a foe he couldn't lick. He was dying of a 'peculiar disease of a peculiar nature.' Had it been tuberculosis the medical authorities would surely have confirmed this diagnosis for posterity. It was a common enough ailment in 19th century America, highly contagious and slowly killed the afflicted. It was a disease that others feared due to its long suffering and ominous ending.

Worried his unknown disease would place others at risk; Bowie asked to be moved from his quarters along the west wall and into the gate building where he was more isolated. He also realized he no longer had the strength to carry out his responsibilities as co-commander and relinquished the full garrison to Travis. Bowie had with him his wife's relatives Gertrudis Navarro and Juana Navarro Alsbury along with at least one slave, and possibly a local curandera (folk healer) known to history as Madame Candelaria. As Bowie was being carried off to the low barrack, he tried to reassure Juana. "Sister, do not be afraid. I leave you with Colonel Travis, Colonel Crockett, and other friends. They are gentlemen and will treat you kindly." With Bowie all but eliminated from active participation in the coming struggle, Travis, ready or not, was now the sole commander of the Alamo.

The last several weeks had been an extraordinary time for the young lawyer-turned-soldier. In spite of having no military experience or formal training, Travis was granted a regular commission as a Lieutenant Colonel of Cavalry. But instead of commanding a regiment of horse-soldiers he was sent to Béxar to serve under Colonel Neill.

Aerial view of Low Barracks,
Main Gate Entrance with
defensive Lunette.

Bowie's room was located just left
of the gate to the East.

The Alamo would occasionally exchange fire with the Mexican batteries. The Alamo church featured a three gun battery firing at its eastern end.

17

James Bowie 1996-1836

Detail, hunting knife (G.L. Foreman Collection)

The Alamo was an artilleryman's dream, but for someone like Travis, who was more at home in the saddle, it was a nightmare. He made it clear to Governor Henry Smith that he was unhappy with his assignment, but the governor just ignored him. When he threatened to resign his commission rather than serve in Béxar, Smith simply ignored him again. In the end, Travis decided to obey his orders like a good soldier and report to San Antonio. Just days after arriving at the Alamo, the inexperienced cavalryman was placed in temporary command of the fort and garrison while Colonel Neill was on furlough. The ensuing confrontation with Jim Bowie over command of the whole garrison had turned ugly, but the two leaders managed to overlook their differences agreeing to a joint command. And if things weren't challenging enough, Santa Anna arrived virtually undetected. Were it not for the grace of God or sheer luck, Travis and 150 men would have been slaughtered as they slept. Fortunately for the careless Texians, fate had other designs and the entire garrison was able to withdraw to the relative safety of the Alamo.

But now, big Jim Bowie was down, rendered helpless by an unknown disease and in no condition to offer his experience or leadership to anyone. With both Colonel Neill and Jim Bowie effectively eliminated from the gathering siege, the men of the Alamo looked to Travis for direction and encouragement. If he had any doubts about his ability to command, he quickly put them aside. He had to. For this young leader...this upstart, was about to go head-to-head with the self-proclaimed "Napoleon of the West" and President of Mexico, General Antonio López de Santa Anna.

Travis had much to do. There was powder and ball, beeves and water (though not enough). Cannon had to be placed in battery and non-combatants moved out of harm's way. The biggest problem was manpower: there were not enough men and Travis set about to get more. He was counting on aid from the colonies. Within days, hopefully, militias from Gonzales, San Felipe, Bastrop, and other settlements, would respond and march to the Alamo. Of course there were always the 400 men under the command of Colonel James W. Fannin at Goliad. Surely he would answer the call.

Trevino House, Travis' Headquarters (from The Illustrated Alamo: 1836)

The non-combatants, including Susannah Dickinson and her 15 month-old daughter Angelina, were sheltered in rooms off the nave of the Alamo church.

Outside the Alamo the Mexicans were busy. They established their first battery in the horseshoe of the San Antonio River with two 8-pounders and a howitzer. The cannons began firing shot at the walls and lobbing shells into the Alamo compound causing the defenders to seek cover.

Later on in the morning, the garrison watched as a small group of Mexican cavalry appeared to be riding in a circle around the Alamo reconnoitring the Texians position. Little did they know that Santa Anna was one of the horsemen. It was not unusual for the General to expose himself to danger in such ways, and on this occasion he rode to "within musket shot of the fort." His reconnaissance complete, Santa Anna returned to his headquarters in town. The defenders on the walls missed an opportunity to score a coup.

As the sun set and the 2nd day of the siege was drawing to a close, Travis returned to his quarters. If the garrison was going to have any chance of surviving the fix they were in, he would have to communicate to all Texians...and perhaps to the whole world. The words must have been floating around in his head all day and they needed to be heard.
He grabbed his quill and began to write possibly the most passionate and profound letter of his young life. When he finished inscribing his stirring words of appeal he handed the missive to Albert Martin and instructed him to ride to Gonzales. It was plenty dark when the courier left the Alamo but he had no trouble finding the road and disappearing into the night.

Coahuila y Tejas Flag
The 2 stars represent the unity of 2 Northern provinces of Mexico.

New Orleans Greys Flag
Outfitted and equipped by investors in New Orleans, several companies of men fought at the Siege of Bexar, with about 20 remaining to fight and die in the Alamo.

Lone Star & Stripes Flag
In use for almost 2 years before the Texas Revolution, this ensign closely resembled the United States flag, and mirrored the sentiment many had about turning Texas into a separate Republic.

Detal, Late 1820s Mexican Shako (Joe Musso Collection)

20

Flags of the Alamo: The Waving Controversy

"...our flag still waves proudly from our walls."
Col. W.B. Travis

The question remains:
which flag was Travis referring to?
It's well documented that at least two flags
were hoisted over the Alamo walls;
the tri-color banner with two gold stars in the center,
and the captured New Orleans Greys ensign
that barely survives today in a Mexico City museum.
Another likely candidate that has persistently
nudged historians is the "Lone Star & Stripes" flag,
considered the de facto banner of the Texas Revolution.
Because of its reference and depiction in several key sites,
it would be likely that this might be the flag that Travis referred to.

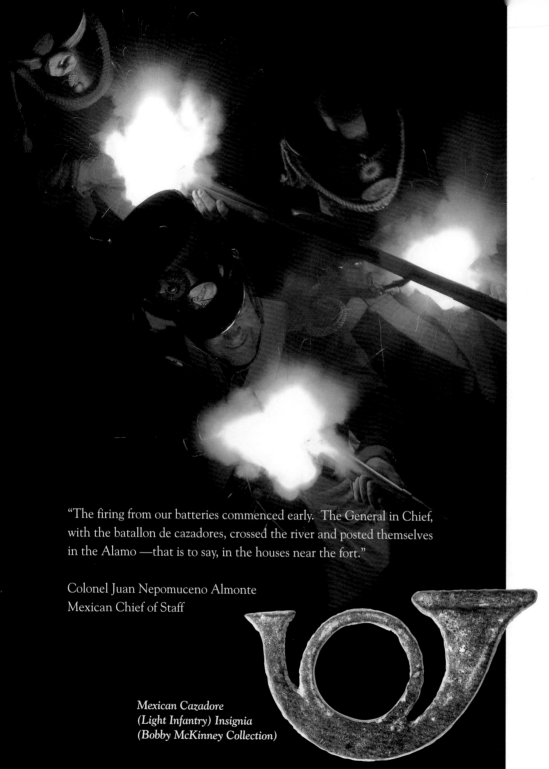

"The firing from our batteries commenced early. The General in Chief, with the batallon de cazadores, crossed the river and posted themselves in the Alamo —that is to say, in the houses near the fort."

Colonel Juan Nepomuceno Almonte
Mexican Chief of Staff

Mexican Cazadore
(Light Infantry) Insignia
(Bobby McKinney Collection)

Day 3 Thursday, February 25

Attack and Repulse

The day broke warmer than the previous day; a welcome change which would have caused soldados from the interior to be grateful. The Mexicans commenced a brisk cannonade at dawn from the two batteries positioned on the west side of the river, and the newest gun emplacement in La Villita. But they needed to do more than lob shells over the Alamo's walls and kick up clods of earth. They needed a foothold on the Alamo side of the San Antonio River. If there was any hope of launching a general assault on the former mission, Santa Anna knew he had to control both sides of the river. The task-organized battalion of cazadores and the Matamoros Permanent Battalion would be the first to engage the Texians in ground combat.

At 9:30 that morning both battalions forded the river. Those soldados with shoes kept them tied together and draped from between the barrel and ramrod of their muskets. The Mexican columns exited the cold water of the San Antonio River leaving behind the neat streets and pastel colors of Béxar, for the mud plastered jacales in La Villita. If Santa Anna was hoping to uncover a weakness, he didn't need to look any further than the barrio or Pueblo de Valero. In their hast to withdraw into the Alamo, the garrison neglected to destroy any of the numerous outbuildings and mud huts that dotted the expanse from the riverbank at La Villita to within 50 yards of the Alamo's south wall. Santa Anna seized upon the opportunity and directed General Manuel Castrillón to advance the columns through the cluster of jacales and attack the Alamo. When the Texians spotted the two enemy battalions, they were moving north from the ford and into the Plaza de Valero. The cry of alarm was sounded and defenders flocked to the south wall, so many in fact, there wasn't enough room on the south ramparts. Men filed out the main gate and jumped down into the surrounding trenches. On the southwest corner artillerymen, possibly Captain's Dickinson and Carey, wheeled the deadly 18-pounder around to meet the threat. The Mexican battalion's closed to "within point blank shot, when we opened a heavy discharge of grape and canister on them," reported Travis, "together with a well directed fire from small arms, which forced them to halt and take shelter in the houses about 90 or 100 yards from our batteries." The intense fire-fight lasted nearly 2 hours after which the bloodied soldados called it a day and withdrew back across the river, taking their dead and wounded with them. During the Mexican retreat, two defenders, Charles Despallier and Robert Brown, darted out of the Alamo "and set fire to the houses which afforded the enemy shelter," wrote Travis, who was justifiably proud of the way his men conducted themselves under fire. In his report to Sam Houston he singled out defenders who, in his judgment, distinguished themselves.

In a probing attack, the cazadores of the Matamoros Battalion move through the jacales of the Pueblo del Álamo and exchange fire with the Alamo garrison.

23

1830s Powder Horn (G.L. Foreman Collection)

David Crockett's behavior and leadership was particularly noteworthy, "The Hon. David Crockett was seen at all points, animating the men to do their duty." The famed frontiersman had become the spirit of the garrison.

Santa Anna learned two things from the day's violent action. First, the norteamericano rebels can project a lot of firepower when defending a single wall...especially when prepared. And second: storming the Alamo was likely to be very costly. He would have to plan more carefully the next time he attacked the Anglos in strength. But Santa Anna had time...and time was on his side. The evening brought darkness and in the blackness of night there was activity from within, and outside the Alamo.

Travis wrote another communiqué. This one was addressed to the commanding general, Sam Houston. After detailing the morning attack and repulse of Santa Anna's battalions, Travis described the seriousness of their situation, "Our numbers are few, and the enemy still continues to approximate his works to ours." Travis could already sense the noose tightening. He requested more men and urged they be sent as quickly as possible, then wrote a prophetic warning, "...as from the superior numbers of the enemy, it will be impossible to keep them out much longer. If they overpower us, we fall a sacrifice at the shrine of our country." He closed the letter with his usual dramatic flair. "...we hope posterity and our country will do our memory justice. Give me help, oh my country! Victory or death!"

Tejano leader and local rancher, Juan Seguín, was elected to carry the letter to Houston. It was reasoned he stood the best chance of clearing the Mexican cavalry patrols now guarding the road. Seguín and his orderly, Antonio Cruz y Arocha, left the Alamo at 8 o'clock in the evening. The pair was stopped on the Gonzales Road by a detachment of lancers, but Seguín convinced them he and Arocha were local ranchers and were allowed to continue on their way.

The Mexicans were anything but idle on this night. Santa Anna ordered another probing attack on the Alamo, but this time he would test the rear defences for signs of weakness. Apparently, the garrison responded to this attack in the same admirable fashion, as Travis wrote, "...we received them gallantly by a discharge of grape shot and musqutery, and they took to their scrapers immediately."

24

The commander in chief, with the companies of cazadores from Jimenez and Matamoros crossed the river and took up a position in the houses and huts to the south of the Alamo about half a rifle shot's distance from the enemy parapets.

In these operations, with the fierce fire from the enemy, we had one corporal and a *cazadore* from Matamoros killed, and four wounded, and two more wounded of those from Jimenez.

Don Vicente Filisola
Mexican General

Indeed, the whole of the men who were brought into action conducted themselves with such heroism that it would be injustice to discriminate. The Hon. David Crockett was seen at all points, animating the men to do their duty. Do hasten on aid to me as rapidly as possible, as from the superior number of the enemy, it will be impossible for us to keep them out much longer.

Victory or Death
W. Barret Travis
Lt.Col. Com[manding]

1815 Kentucky Rifle, Southern Horn,
Shot Pouch (Ric Lambert Photography)

25

To the south of the Alamo along the Alameda, a section of road that bisected a grove of massive cottonwood trees, Mexican engineers were busy preparing entrenchments for the Matamoras Battalion who were recently tasked with guarding this stretch of road. East of the tree-lined Alameda Santa Anna posted the Dolores Regiment (reinforced) at the Powder House on the Gonzales Road. The Mexicans now controlled the vital lifeline from the colonies to the Alamo. The noose was indeed tightening.

At Fort Defiance, the fortified mission at Goliad, Colonel James Walker Fannin had come to a decision. He heard Travis' appeal for aid and concluded he must answer the call. "I am aware that my present movement toward Béxar is anything but a military one", he wrote to Lieutenant Governor James Robinson, "The appeal of cols Travis & Bowie cannot however pass unnoticed…Much must be risked to relieve the besieged." Fannin would march towards the Alamo the next morning, leading 320 men, 4 cannon, and several wagons carrying supplies, and leave 80 to 100 men to garrison Fort Defiance.

Mexicans and Americans alike remember Santa Anna for many evils and precious little altruism. One of his many sins was that of lechery if not polygamy. There was a Béxareña who caught his eye during the battle of this date: 17-year-old Senorita Melchora Iniega Barrera. She lived with her widowed mother in the barrios of Béxar. Colonel Miñón, who knew Santa Anna's tastes and desired to curry favour with the president-general, noted the girl. Though destitute and living in a hovel, her mother had some pride and said she was from a good family and refused Santa Anna to have access to her daughter except through nuptials, so a plan was decided on. All he needed was a faux priest. Miñón had such a man in his command and the officer borrowed vestments and other items necessary to pull off the stunt. The false wedding took place later in the siege and the honeymoon lasted until the Army of the North left San Antonio in March. The girl was sent to San Luis Postosi in the interior, where she was placed in care of a fine family and eventually bore a son.

West Wall of the Alamo. Seguin followed the acequia past enemy lines.
(from The Illustrated Alamo: 1836)

On the night of the 25th, Juan Seguin and Antonio Cruz y Arocha depart, most likely by the northern postern, carrying a verbal message to Fannin at Goliad.

"…[T]wo companies were sent to make a reconnaissance. They went within range of the deadly rifle, thirty [soldados] were killed within a few minutes."

Francisco Becerra
1st Sergeant, Active San Luis Battalion

Day 4 Friday, February 26

Cold Wind and Low Water

The cold was becoming somewhat of a problem. An icy north wind or Blue Norther which had arrived the night prior, was pummelling the combatants on both sides and drawing-off precious body heat. But it wasn't just the freezing wind; the walls, the weapons, and the ground siphoned heat as well. The cold, muddy earth in the entrenchments around the Alamo dampened the Mexicans keeping them wet from the knees down. The cold had created miserable living conditions and caused indiscriminate suffering in Texian and soldado, alike.

Water. It had been a wet winter, but one cannot drink mud which was all there was in the Alamo, besides the tiny well near the convento. A healthy adult can survive a while without food, but not water, and after 4 days of siege (and no doubt drinking small amounts of rationed water) the circumstances forced the Texians' hand. Since the Alamo's well was lacking, Travis sent out an armed party to fetch water from the acequia just east of the corrals. The cold likely brought more volunteers than needed to venture out of the relative safety of the Alamo. The action would also prove to their besiegers that neither Nature nor Mexican soldados could intimidate them.

General of Brigade Ramírez y Sesma commanded a task force of the Dolores Cavalry Regiment, cazadores, and the Matamoros Battalion entrenched near the Alameda. Knowing the layout of the Alamo and realizing one tiny well could not provide the Texians with enough water, he probably deployed his forces with an eye toward the eastern acequia. When the Texians sallied out from the Alamo he had his cazadores ready to meet them. As night fell the Texians shifted their focus from the East towards the South. Travis sent the raiding party out again to burn the remaining jacales in Plaza de Valero. During one of these night battles Colonel Juan Maria Bringas was ordered to lead his men in a counterattack over the bridge but the hot Texian fire forced him to retreat to safety.

Looking NE: Long Barracks and flooded acequia. The well in front of the Convento was not sufficient for drawing water, so the defenders made water runs directly outside their walls to the East, often drawing enemy fire and attacks.
(from The Illustrated Alamo: 1836)

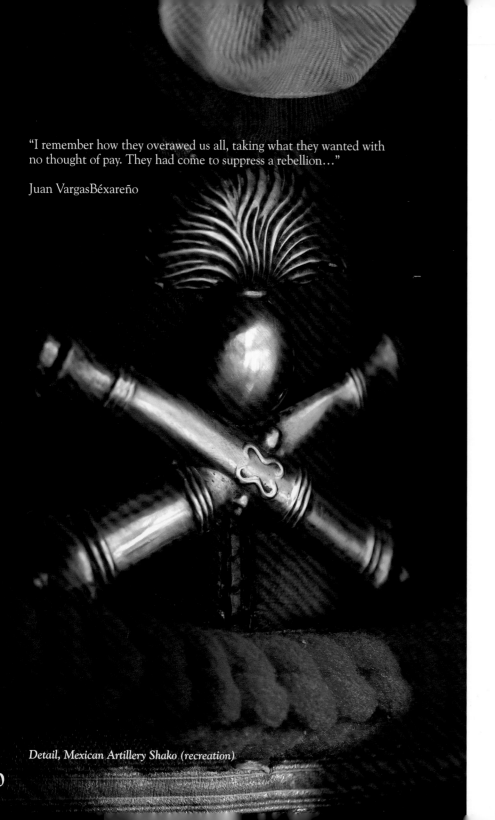

"I remember how they overawed us all, taking what they wanted with no thought of pay. They had come to suppress a rebellion…"

Juan VargasBéxareño

Detail, Mexican Artillery Shako (recreation)

Day 5 Saturday, February 27

Tightening the Noose

The 5th day of the siege began like the previous one – cold and very windy. The temperature rose to a high of 39° but the strong Norther breeze made it feel much colder. The defenders in the Alamo continued with their daily routine of watching the surrounding terrain for movement (either friendly or hostile), huddling by a warm fire, sniping at the entrenched Mexicans, and fortifying the walls. The north wall was a primary concern.

When the Mexican army occupied the fort in the fall of 1835, they addressed the decaying north wall by strengthening it with a thick outer reinforcement of earth and timber. But the Mexicans were forced out before the repair work could be completed, and the Texians never got around to finishing the job when they moved in. So now, with the Mexicans erecting new batteries and drawing their siege lines tighter, the garrison labored to fortify the weakened north perimeter and hoped it would be enough to keep the enemy from breaking through. The defenders were under no illusions; they knew if Santa Anna's legions penetrated the outer wall, all would be lost.

North of the Alamo, the Mexicans were engaged with activities of their own. Santa Anna instructed his engineers to cut off the supply of water to the rebels by damming the acequia that fed the Alamo. From the walls, the Texians watched as a small group of Mexicans made their way to the ditch and began their work. It didn't take long for the defenders to figure out what was going on. Riflemen steadied their long guns and took pot shots at the enemy laborers. Meanwhile, Travis ordered a new well to be dug in case the Mexicans were successful. The anxiety proved to be unnecessary as the frustrated engineers were unable to block the acequia and stop the flow of water. The whole spectacle may have even provided the garrison with some momentary laughter.

Brass 4 pounder cannon similar to the arsenal at the Alamo

Mission Concepcion. Mexican troops filed past these walls during the Alamo siege in search of possible reinforcements coming up the Goliad Road.

31

Supplying enough food for hundreds of soldiers was a daunting task and Santa Anna's army was running low on provisions. Lieutenant Manuel Menchacho was directed to form a foraging detail and gather all the cattle, hogs, and corn he could from some of the local ranches, two in particular. The soldados rode down the Goliad Road past the 4 other missions and followed the San Antonio River to forage at the Erasmo Seguín's rancho and the Rancho Los Chayopines belonging to Francisco Flores de Abrego y Valdes (both near present Graytown). Both Seguín and Flores opposed the President-General and were labelled as enemies.

On this day, Santa Anna called for new entrenchments to be excavated and he wanted them closer. He also ordered the battery in La Villita to be positioned nearer to the south wall. As darkness fell, "His Excellency" instructed the engineers to construct a new gun emplacement to the northeast of the mission and west of acequia del Alamo. At first light the next morning the garrison would awake to see the new threat.

This two cannon battery on the NW corner, known as Fortin de Condelle, would be the target for General Cos' column. This is one of the locations where Travis may have been killed in the final attack. (from The Illustrated Alamo: 1836)

Alamo Compound, as seen above from the NW looking SE. In the foreground is the North Wall where the bulk of the Mexican final attack would take place. (from The Illustrated Alamo: 1836)

The Defenders: Who were they?

They were ordinary men poised to do extraordinary things. They were common folk; cut from the same cloth but uniquely different. Their individual faces, occupations, and personal stories, were as diverse as their clothing and as wide-ranging as their dreams. Perhaps their love of freedom was the common bond, or maybe it was their vision of Texas. Whatever it was, it brought them all to the Alamo and they were willing to fight and die for it. They were mostly Southerners, but there were many from the northern states as well as seven native-born Texans, and a score who journeyed to Texas from the old countries across the Atlantic. All rugged individuals who just wanted to live their lives free from an over-reaching government. They were doctors, lawyers, shopkeepers, ranchers, farmers, blacksmiths, preachers, hunters, adventurers, and one former U.S. Congressmen. A few had military experience, but most had never donned a uniform. They were not true soldiers, and contrary to popular belief, they weren't all "crack shots". Some didn't even own a gun, but that wasn't going to keep them from fighting for liberty.

The average age of those defending the Alamo was 28.
The oldest was 56 year old Gordon C. Jennings.
The youngest in the garrison may have been William King, who at age 15 was barely old enough to shave.
More than a few entered the Alamo with their families.
Almeron Dickinson brought his wife Susanna, and their 15 month old baby girl, Angelina.
James Bowie had his wife's cousins with him.
Gregorio Esparza was accompanied by his wife, Ana, and their 4 children. Anthony Wolfe took his 2 boys, Benjamin and Michael, into the mission, and they may have played with young Enrique Esparza.
For Toribio Losoya's family, the Alamo had been their home and it seemed the proper place for them to be.
His mother, younger brother and sister would survive the bloody battle, but Toribio was killed. His body found just a short distance from where he was born.

Day 6 Sunday, February 28

Hope Begins to Fade

Colonel James Fannin turned around.

The choice he made was due to meager resolve and sloppy preparations. He had left one company of regular infantry to garrison Fort Defiance (like the Alamo, another Texian fort guarding the roads into the colonies) and marched the remaining 320 toward San Antonio to relieve the Alamo siege. They had only traversed one mile when it all fell apart. In fording the San Antonio River, 3 ox drawn wagons broke down and 4 cannon finally made it across. Eventually the command made it to the opposite bank, all except for the ammunition wagon.

The Goliad men were not the raggedymen of the Alamo, but better uniformed and better drilled soldiers. As they marched out of the gate, the long line of mostly uniformed soldiery marched in columns of 4 out to the great adventure: Alabama Red Rovers, San Antonio Greys, Louisville Volunteers, Kentucky Mustangs from Bardstown, the Georgia Battalion, and the Mobile Greys. That night across the river, the oxen were not hobbled and they wandered off looking for forage. Search parties could not locate the animals. As is common in populist wars of liberty, a war council convened and the situation was regarded as embarrassing in the least, and starvation at the worst. Others may have soldiered on; force marching to San Antonio and surely this size force would have made a difference in the assault that was to come on March 6th. But that was not Fannin—he could be excused for this, after all Fannin was not to relieve the Alamo if Goliad was attacked—that was the duty of the colonial militia. Fannin was to guard the eastern approaches to the colonies for the force they knew would be coming up the Coastal Road. What to do?

"News was received that a reinforcement was coming by the road from la Bahia, in number 200. It was not true."

Colonel Juan Nepomuceno Almonte
Mexican Chief of Staff

Chapel, Presidio La Bahia, Goliad (Glenn Effler Photo)

34

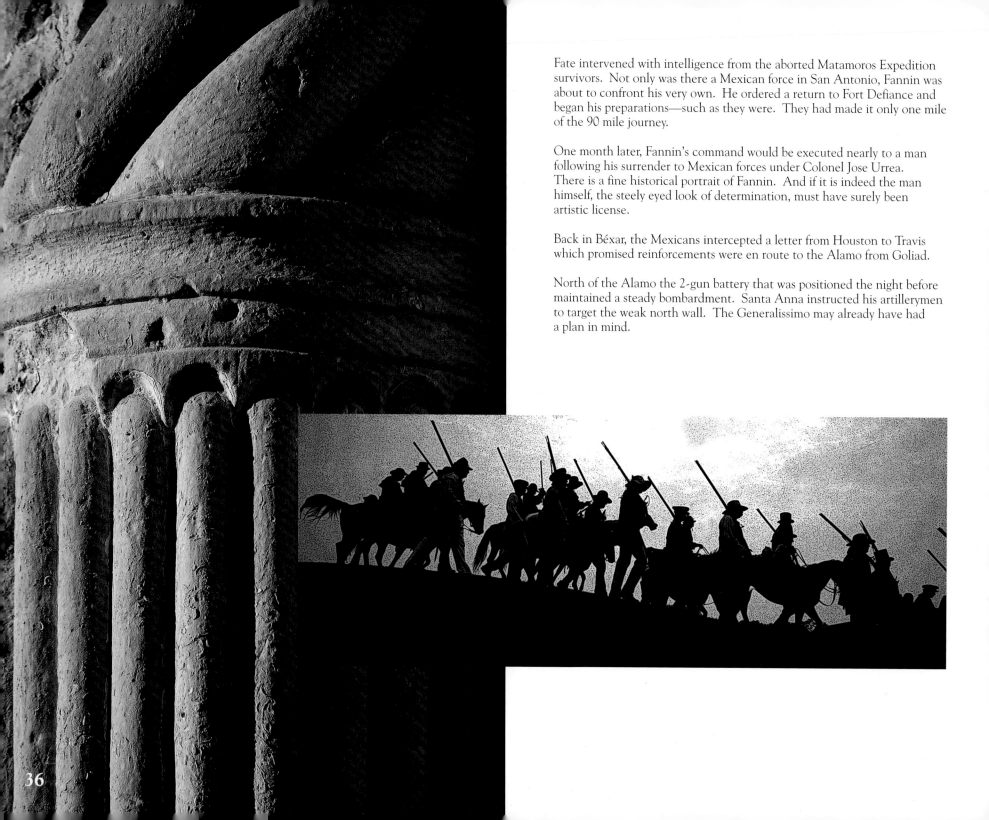

Fate intervened with intelligence from the aborted Matamoros Expedition survivors. Not only was there a Mexican force in San Antonio, Fannin was about to confront his very own. He ordered a return to Fort Defiance and began his preparations—such as they were. They had made it only one mile of the 90 mile journey.

One month later, Fannin's command would be executed nearly to a man following his surrender to Mexican forces under Colonel Jose Urrea. There is a fine historical portrait of Fannin. And if it is indeed the man himself, the steely eyed look of determination, must have surely been artistic license.

Back in Béxar, the Mexicans intercepted a letter from Houston to Travis which promised reinforcements were en route to the Alamo from Goliad.

North of the Alamo the 2-gun battery that was positioned the night before maintained a steady bombardment. Santa Anna instructed his artillerymen to target the weak north wall. The Generalissimo may already have had a plan in mind.

Fiddle & Bagpipes: The Alamo Serenade

"Colonel Crockett was a performer on the violin, and often during the siege took it up and played his favorite tunes."

Susannah Dickinson
Alamo Survivor

Throughout the decades, the speculation has grown that during lulls in the Alamo siege, music was performed in rustic fashion by Scotsman John McGregor on the bagpipes, and David Crockett with his fiddle and bow. Although only some claimed the musical dual actually took place, popular culture has traditionally carried the story quite well, for almost two centuries. If it is fact, one can only imagine how it was received within hearing distance beyond the Alamo walls.

David Crockett's Tennessee Fiddle (Witte Museum Collection)

The Alamo's Coahuila y Tejas flag was seen by eye-witnesses at least 3 different times during the siege.

Day 7 Monday, February 29

The Truce

The temperature slackened a bit and the low was 40° at morning, though there is no telling what the wind made of the warming. At first blush, little happened on this date at the Alamo, but such a view fails upon closer inspection. After Juan Seguín left with Travis' message for Fannin, a change occurred within the garrison. Not a great out-crying, no arguments, nothing that is recorded in the historical record, aside from brief mention in mostly academic studies of the siege. A number of Tejanos left the Alamo this day. Perhaps they had good reason.
Perhaps they felt pressured in some silent way by being enclosed by their countrymen, to sit and wait to die alongside Anglos who shared neither their religion nor vision of what they struggled for. Perhaps they thought it a losing battle and determined to fight another day, or perhaps they were disheartened by the departure of their leader.

There is one occurrence that could have motivated the Tejanos to make the decisions they did. Santa Anna appealed to his native born countrymen in the Alamo, offering a 3 day truce, where those inside the fort could withdraw safely, if they surrendered arms and took an oath to his government.

In Béxar, the intelligence from the day before caused the Mexicans to send a detachment of the Jiménez Battalion and the Dolores Cavalry Regiment from their positions near the Alameda and reconnoitre down the Goliad Road. Their orders were to find the suspected Goliad column, and arrange it so they attacked the reinforcements at dawn for best effect. Santa Anna added a notorious postscript to the orders and reminded General of Brigade Ramírez y Sesma that there were to be no prisoners in this war.

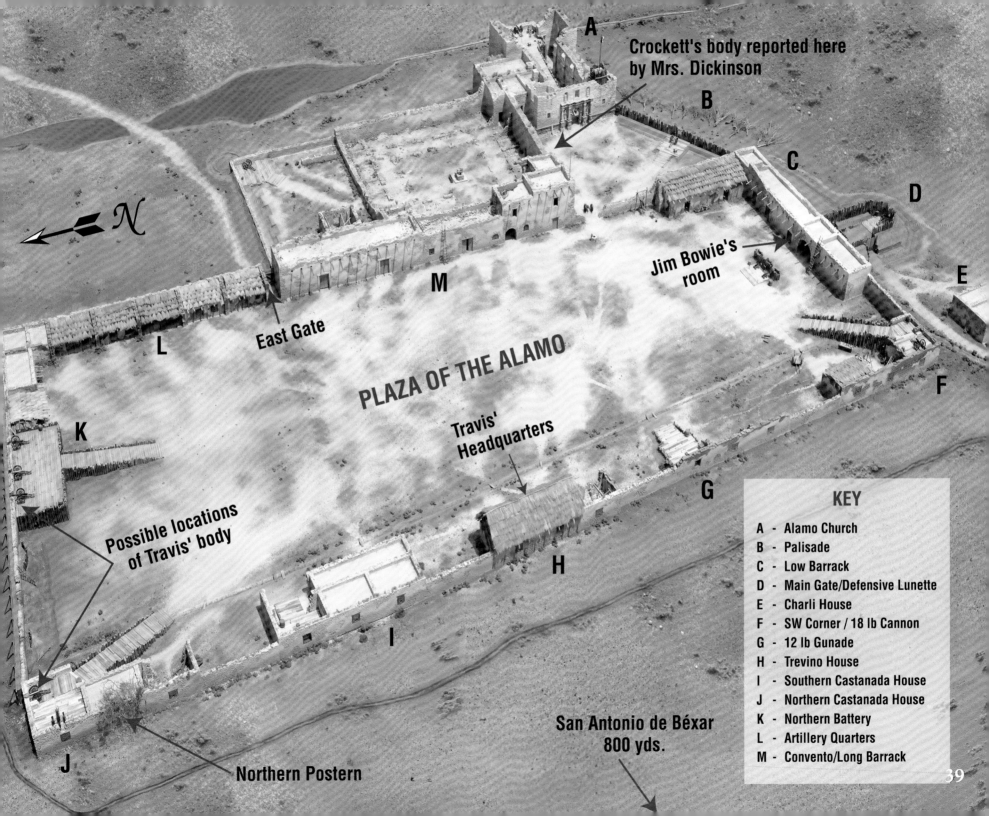

A — Crockett's body reported here by Mrs. Dickinson

B

C

D

E

F

G

H

N

Jim Bowie's room

East Gate

M

L

PLAZA OF THE ALAMO

Travis' Headquarters

K

Possible locations of Travis' body

I

J

Northern Postern

San Antonio de Béxar 800 yds.

KEY

A - Alamo Church
B - Palisade
C - Low Barrack
D - Main Gate/Defensive Lunette
E - Charli House
F - SW Corner / 18 lb Cannon
G - 12 lb Gunade
H - Trevino House
I - Southern Castanada House
J - Northern Castanada House
K - Northern Battery
L - Artillery Quarters
M - Convento/Long Barrack

Texian Defenders

New Orleans Grey **Colonist** **Volunteer** **Backwoodsman** **Cavalryman**

The men inside the walls of the Alamo probably resembled a scene more likely from a Charles Dickens play than the popular culture image of the American Mountain Man that many hold today. Desperately pressed into action without much supplies or extra clothing, many suffered from the winter of 1835-36, considered one of the worst during the early 19th century. Although the popular hunting shirt of buckskin, wool, or linen was worn, the gentleman's fashion of the day prevailed almost everywhere, including tailcoats, frock coats, vests, and cravats. The only "uniform" of the garrison was that of the New Orleans Greys, wearing a simple grey "roundabout" jacket and trousers, a cap with visor and either a rifle or musket.

Mexican Forces

Rifleman　　　**Regular Cavalry**　　　**Grenadier**　　　**Regular Infantry**　　　**Infantry Officer**

The Mexican army that crossed the Rio Grande into Texas with Santa Anna was clothed and equipped with a wide variety of different military issues. Some of the Soldados were wearing the older vintage uniforms from the last days of the Spanish regime of the 1820s to the latest patterns of the early 1830s. Most were equipped with British weapons, including the Brown Bess muskets and Baker Rifles. Some accounts and archeological evidence suggest that a good number of late 18th century Spanish muskets were also carried by various regiments. While the preferred or elite companies received shoes, many wore sandals throughout the bitter Texas campaign.

Day 8 Tuesday, March 1

Help From Gonzales

One man returned.
Albert Martin was no kin of anyone in Texas and was from a place few of the Alamo defenders had ever heard of, and if they had, it would have taken a debate to convince them that Rhode Island was not really an island, and it was really a state in the Union. Martin had served at the Battle of Gonzales and then marched with the Texian Army of the People to take San Antonio from General Cós. On the 2nd day, he had been sent by Travis to rally men to Béxar, so he had missed most of the Alamo siege.

A hole. A gap. There are risks to every decision made on a battlefield. The day prior, Santa Anna had ordered the reinforced cavalry regiment of Dolores to Mission San Francisco de la Espada to prevent a suspected re-inforcement from Goliad. He replaced them in the siege lines with the re-mainder Jiménez Battalion not reconnoitring with General Ramírez y Sesma. But an infantry battalion can be a poor choice compared to an adept cavalry unit.

There was no Wordsworth or Tennyson to glorify their ride, no light in Boston's North Church to motivate the "32", rather they answered Travis' simple request for help. The Gonzales Mounted Ranging Company had started from Gonzales for the Alamo on February 27th, with Alamo couriers Albert Martin in command and John Sutherland as their guide. Though labelled as the Lexington of the Texas Revolution, this comparison is not entirely apropos. Gonzales citizens were not the agitated New Eng-landers of their parents' war, but rather counted moderation as a virtue, naming their town after Governor Rafael Gonzáles in an effort to prove their loyalty to their new homeland. The town acted as the capital of the De Witt Colony. They had been moderates and stayed away from the rousing calls for revolution raised in the interior colonies until September 10th, when the popular sheriff, Jesse McCoy (who would also ride to the Alamo) was musket whipped by a soldado in Adam Zumwalt's Gonzales storeroom. If that weren't enough to turn the moderate citizens into insurgents, 3 weeks later the Mexicans sent a company of presidiales to the town and ordered the cannon, given to them for defence against Indians, be returned. The Gonzales citizens made a flag with a simple cannon on it and the words: "Come and Take it" written above the cannon with a single lone star between them.

"A company of thirty-two men from Gonzales, made their way into us on the morning of the 1st inst., at three o'clock."

William Barret Travis
Lieutenant Colonel, Alamo Commandant

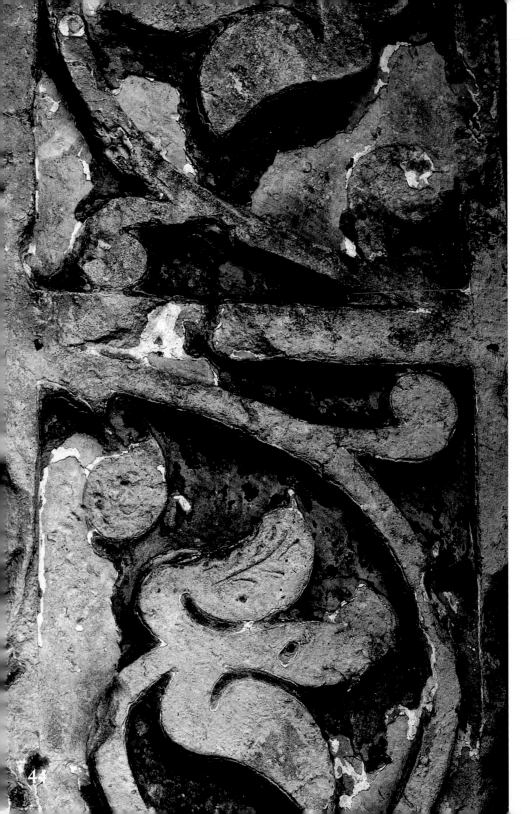

When they got close to the Alamo they broke north from the Gonzales Road somewhere before the Powder House with its entrenchments and soldados screening the road from the Anglo colonies. They broke chaparral and scrub oaks, knowing every twig snap, creak of leather, or horse's cough could bring lancers down upon them. The temperature was 36° and they were wide awake regardless of the early morning hour and the near full moon. This clear, cold and cloudless evening would not have given them anymore confidence. Though they would soon be discovered, they must have managed a bit of satisfaction when they finally saw the white walls of the Alamo reflected in the moon light.

They were approached by a single man on horse back. They halted and he asked them, in English, if they needed to enter the Alamo. They affirmed, but soon enough skulduggery was suspected and John Smith shouted out to kill their guide as he rode away without an explanation that would have come from a compatriot. The men from Gonzales rode on and eventually entered the Alamo.

Long Barracks, looking SE across Alamo Plaza. The passageway at the far left end of this 2-story structure is believed to be the East Gate Entrance used by the Gonzales 32 and courier James Butler Bonham.

45

"Let the convention go on and make a declaration of independence, and we will then understand, and the world will understand, what we are fighting for...[U]nder the flag of independence, we are ready to peril our lives a hundred times a day, and to drive away the monster who is fighting us under a blood-red flag, threatening to murder all prisoners and make Texas a waste desert."

William Barret Travis
Lieutenant Colonel, Alamo Commandant

Day 9 Wednesday, March 2

Texas Becomes a Republic

Washington Town, Robertson's Colony

The men at the Alamo could have told you who they were fighting against, but would have become argumentative trying to explain what they were fighting for. Some distance north and east that question was being answered for them.

It had only been incorporated one year prior and was laid out on the west side of the Brazos near the mouth of the Navasota River. Washington Town had no romantic views or history particular to note it as a place of liberty. There was an inn present but it filled quickly and the majority of the delegates had to make do with whatever accommodations they could find. For many whose lives intersected here, Washington became the destination for presenting difficult situations and owning up to tougher choices. Those who habitually lived on the edge found there way here. Bowie, Travis, Crockett and Houston all knew this town. Now others took their place to resolve the dramatic issues at hand. Despite the alarming situations, most believed the Alamo was secure.

The delegates who arrived at this potter's field were of one mind. There would be no more emissaries or Olive Branch petitions. They met at 9 o'clock that morning and it was the 2nd day of the convention. What the delegates at Washington Town determined for prosperity was the 'why' of the Texian War for Independence. 51 men squeezed into a building that was as cold within, as without. Gunsmith, Noah Turner Byars leased the vacant building to middlemen in hopes that the exclusive gathering might attract growth and respectability. The building was one of only 3 in town with wooden floors and milled wood siding; the town's remainder being log cabins and palisades. The building had neither finished windows nor doors and cotton was stretched across the openings to temper the wind.

No printing press existed in Washington Town, so secretaries were appointed to encourage the text and send it to the other colonies.

Here is a small selection:

"When a government has ceased to protect the lives, liberty and property of the people, from whom its legitimate powers are derived [...] We therefore, the delegates [...] of the people of Texas [...] do hereby resolve and Declare that our political connection with the Mexican nation has forever ended, and that the people of Texas, do now constitute a Free, Sovereign, and independent Republic and are freely invested with all the rights and attributes which properly belong to independent nations and conscious of the rectitude of our intentions, we fearlessly and confidently commit the issue to the decision of the supreme Arbiter of the destinies of nations"

Independence Hall, Washington-on-the-Brazos State Park. This recreated structure stands on the approximate site of the original wood planked building.

They called on God and drew from John Locke and declared themselves a free nation. There was no debate on the wordings of the declaration, penned by George Childress, and all delegates voted in favour with no amendments within an hour of hearing it the first time. What choice had they? There were only 2 forts of armed colonists and one was already besieged. This was now war. Childress made one other significant contribution by resolving that Texian soldiers wear a Lone Star on their hats.

As the Mexicans probed for weaknesses in the Alamo's defense, and looked forward to the arrival of fresh reinforcements, the besieged Texians had no way of knowing about the events that gave meaning to what they were about to die for.

Detail, quill writing pens

Texas Declaration of Independence (Texas State Library & Archives)

Original Ferry Crossing, Washington-on-the-Brazos State Park. Old wagons ruts and worn horse trails from the early 19th century remain quite visible today.

49

Day 10 Thursday, March 3

Alamo Couriers

Major James Butler Bonham, former Lieutenant Colonel of the South Carolina militia and organizer of Fannin's Mobile Greys (who by now had returned to their company street at Goliad) rode into the Alamo unmolested at around 11 o'clock that morning. He had been gone 3 weeks, sent by Travis with a message to Colonel Fannin, and had last seen San Antonio on the 16th of February. From Goliad, Bonham headed northeast, possibly to San Felipe and then to Washington-on-the-Brazos. On March 1st, Jim Bonham was in Gonzales. By this time, he was undoubtedly aware of the arrival of the Mexican army in San Antonio, and that his comrades in the Alamo were probably surrounded. Also in Gonzales was Travis' friend, Robert Williamson, who was there organizing relief for the Béxar garrison. Upon hearing that Bonham was returning to the Alamo, he quickly drafted a letter to be delivered to Travis. "Sixty men have left this municipality, who in all probability are with you at this date." Were the 32 men from Gonzales that entered the Alamo on March 1st, part of the "sixty men" Williamson referred to, or were there two separate groups? No one knows for sure. Williamson's letter promised hundreds more men were marching to aid the besieged. In closing, Williamson writes, "For God's sake hold out until we can assist you." Bonham took the letter and rode west, determined to report to Travis "or die in the attempt." Across the river reinforcements did arrive—for the Mexicans. Colonel Francisco Duque acting commander of the 1st brigade of General of Brigade Gaona's division arrived with almost 1,000 soldados including the elite Zapadores Battalion (used for attacking fortified places) and 2 artillery pieces. They had been hurried on by Santa Anna as of the 27th of February and the units that arrived had force marched 120 miles in 5 days. They would have been exhausted and little use for direct action. The total number of soldados in Béxar now numbered 2,370 against about 200 or more Texians.

Indeed, March 3rd had become the reckoning day when all the final chess moves were lodging into place. Regardless, perhaps some of the most important pieces of history came from the Travis letters, carried away by one of the last Alamo couriers, John W. Smith (who would become a future San Antonio mayor). The dramatic writings not only declare the sober realities facing the Alamo defenders, it reveals Travis' personal transformation as a selfless patriot who had quickly matured beyond his 26 years of life.

"One night there was music in the Mexican camp and the Mexican prisoner said it meant that reinforcements had arrived."

Enrique Esparza
Alamo non-combatant

Mexican Grenaderos (Grenadiers) displayed in Parade/Battle Dress and white cotton Fatigue/Camp Dress. A surviving diary from a Mexican officer describes how the large column arriving in Bexar on March 3rd halted just outside of town and changed from their fatigues into parade uniforms prior to reaching the main camp. These uniforms represent how earlier styles from the previous decade were mixed in with updated versions.

Battalion Guerrero brass plate & Spanish Coins (Johnnie Bubenik Collection)

"..the subject of what to do with prisoners was brought up…
the example of [Joaquín de] Arrendondo was cited:
during the Spanish rule he had hanged 800 or more
colonists after having triumphed in a military action,
and this conduct was taken as a model."

José Enrique de la Peña
Lieutenant Colonel, Mexican Staff

"The enemy attempted a sally in the night…
but were repulsed by our advance."

Col. J. Almonte

Day 11 Friday, March 4

A Council of War

Night. Windy and cold.

Santa Anna chaired a lengthy council of war. There were many arguments for and against attacking the Alamo, but caution prevailed and the council determined to wait until the next brigade arrived on the 7th to press matters with the Texians. Prisoners: The President-General brought up the subject of prisoners, but not in how to care for them, or where to corral them, and when (or if) to parole them. This discussion, if it can be called such, was over the execution of prisoners. He wanted to test the resolve of his fellow officers regarding their abhorrence at the idea of summary execution of the defenceless. All were pirates and to be dealt with accordingly.

While awaiting the arrival of the final brigade to storm the Alamo, something happened. It came from within the Alamo: A Tejana left the garrison. There were a few in the Alamo who had stayed with their husbands or extended family inside the walls, but one of them changed the course of history. She told the Mexicans all about the goings on in the Alamo, advancing the Mexican timetable by 2 days. The general assault would now take place on the 6th. The Mexican batteries moved closer during the night.

Was it a skirmish or something else? In recent years, Alamo historians have revisited original statements regarding the late hours between March 3rd and 4th, some suggesting that a substantial group of Texian reinforcements broke through enemy lines and brought the actual number of defenders to around 250, which correlates with some key Mexican accounts. Did the Williamson letter prompt Travis to send someone out 20 miles southeast to the Cibolo River Crossing, in present-day LaVernia, to guide the desperately needed numbers to the Alamo? Several accounts say it was none other than David Crockett and two others who rendezvoused with the mounted troop and rode under a bright moon to the besieged fortress.

"My soldiers, I am going to meet the fate that becomes me.
Those who will stand by me, let them remain,
but those who desire to go, let them".

William Barret Travis
Lieutenant Colonel, Alamo Commandant

Fact or Legend: Travis draws the line.

Day 12 Saturday, March 5

The Line

A siege is a form of strangulation and the Texians inside the walls of the
Alamo must have sensed that their world was beginning to cave in.
The Mexican battery on the north had advanced much closer and was de-
livering a "brisk fire" from 6 artillery pieces. Later in the day, Mexican gen-
erals could be seen with their escorts, analyzing various locations for their
planned attack. The time had come for facing that final reality.

There are accounts which tell of a great moment of despair inside the
Alamo: When Travis gathered his men around him and explained that no
more help would be forthcoming in time to rescue them. He referenced for
them the Mexican's flag of "no quarter" flying from the belfry of the San
Fernando Church 800 yards away, and reminded them of stories from the
recent past where thousands of Zacatecans had been executed following
their abortive federalist revolt against the centralist usurper Santa Anna.
There was always the chance of escape, though slim, with a regiment of
cavalry on the Gonzales Road—the road home. Surrender and mercy was a
forlorn hope. The last option left to the men was one of arms, as they had
done up to this moment, to kill as many soldados as could be done when
the time came. Then, according to one account, Travis drew a line and
asked all who would, to step across the line and join him in death.
All crossed, but two. Jim Bowie asked that his cot be carried across the line.
The other may have been a man named Louis 'Moses' Rose, who
claimed to have been a soldier of Napoleon's Grand Armee and a survivor
of the failed Russian Campaign. Rose refused to cross and climbed the wall,
leaving the men to their fate.

Some time that night, Travis removed
his opal mourning ring and strung it
as a necklace for little Angelina Dick-
enson, daughter of one of his artillery
officers. James Allen would have been
preparing to ride as the
final courier out of the fort.

*Detail, cuff of Col. Morales uniform
(San Jacinto Battlefield Museum Collection)*

There is rarely historical forethought
in men. When in a crisis the natural
desire is to avoid it, and it is too rarely understood that the upcoming Cru-
cible was the moment they had been born for.

At midnight, the Mexicans awakened.

*On the afternoon of March 5th, Santa Anna and Colonel Morales reconnoitered
a possible route of approach for the dawn assault.*

Detail, Dragoon helmet plate (Joe Musso Collection)

Mexican Organization for Battle

1st Column
Commander: General Cós
Aldama Permanent Battalion (6 fusilero and 1 cazadores companies)
San Luis Active Battalion (1st, 2nd and 3rd fusilero companies)
10 ladders, 2 crowbars and 2 axes

2nd Column
Commander: Colonel Duque
Toluca Active Battalion (6 fusilero and 1 cazadores companies)
San Luis Active Battalion (4th, 5th and 6th fusilero companies)
10 ladders

3rd Column
Commander: Colonel José María Romero
Matamoros Permanent Battalion (6 fusilero companies)
Jiménez Permanent Battalion (6 fusilero companies)
6 ladders

4th Column
Commander: Colonel Juan Morales
Provisional Cazadore Battalion (cazadore companies from the Jiménez, Matamoros and San Luis Battalions)

Reserve Column
Lieutenant Colonel Agustín Amat
Zapadores Battalion
Provisional Granadero Battalion (granadero companies from Matamoros, Jiménez, Aldama, Toluca and San Luis Battalions)

Cavalry
General Joaquín Ramírez y Sesma
Dolores Permanent Regiment
Veracruz Active Platoon
Coahuila Active Company
Río Grande Presidial Company

Early 19th century Howitzer replica (John Destatte Collection)

Late 18th or 19th century Crucifix, found near original
Mexican retreat route (Johnnie Bubenik Collection).

"Keep this for me" Sensing the end was near, Travis removed his cat's eye ring, ran a piece
of string through it and placed it around 15 month old Angelina Dickinson's neck.

"I am determined to perish in the defence of this place, and my bones shall reproach my country for her neglect."

William Barret Travis
Lieutenant Colonel, Alamo Commandant

Day 13 Sunday, March 6

The Crucible

The fateful day began at 1 o'clock in the morning, the night temperature dropping to about 40° with just enough wind to give some lift to the silk Mexican battalion flags that had been unsheathed. The moon was almost full but a cloud cover, as one officer recalled, "Concealed the design of impending death". The Mexican army was now forming into their assault columns under a surreal shroud of absolute silence, as guides met them in their marshalling areas and brought them to their positions.

Detail, Col. Morales uniform
(San Jacinto Battlefield Museum Collection)

The attacking columns to the north and east converged and enveloped the northern end of the compound, overwhelming the defenses and sealing the garrison's fate.

The first attack column of 355 hundred soldados (fusiliers and rifleman) was commanded by General Cós. He would attack and overwhelm the northwest corner and the two cannon that guarded the position. The last time General Cós had seen the Alamo was in December of the previous year when he was forced to surrender the town and the fortress during the Battle of Béxar. He had vowed never to take up arms against the 1824 Constitution or Texas and was paroled back to Mexico. The General now stood just 200 hundred yards outside the Alamo in violation of his promise and waited to avenge his humiliation.

Attack on NW corner. "General Cos, looking for a starting point from which to climb, had advanced frontally with his column to where the second and third were."

Jose Enrique de la Pena

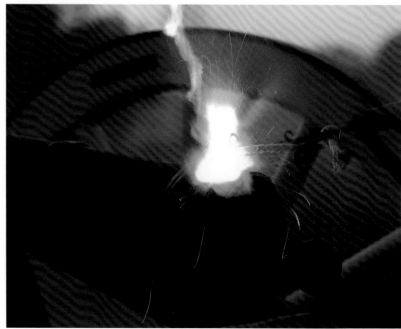

General Cós ordered his men to execute an oblique maneuver, and then wheeled them around towards the sparsely defended west wall.

The second column of 395 soldados (fusiliers and rifleman) was commanded by Colonel Francisco Duque. This column was ordered to storm the north wall and the 3-gun battery at its center. Colonel Jose Maria Romero would lead the third assault column of 300 fusiliers against the low wall of the northeast courtyard. And finally, Colonel Juan Morales would command the fourth column of 120 cazadores and capture the south gate and the defensive lunette. Some of the assault columns would be issued axes and crowbars to batter down barred doors or blocked windows; all were provided with scaling ladders.

Cannister balls, discarded on Mexican retreat (Bobby McKinney Collection)

Climbing up north wall. "The most daring of our veterans tried to be the first to climb... The first to climb were thrown down by bayonets already waiting for them behind the parapet, or by pistol fire."

Jose Enrique de la Pena

Fierce fighting at the north wall became hand to hand until the dwindling number of Texians was compelled to fall back.

63

Mexican Flag replica (Adam Dominguez / Martin Vasquez Collection)

3:00 AM. Once in position and without benefit of blanket or cloak, the soldados laid down to fitfully sleep on the cold earth that sucked the heat out of their bodies. If the Texians could have seen them, it would have looked like a great living red and blue carpet encircling the Alamo, with patches of foggy breath rising, each shifting about to keep in as much warmth as possible. For two agonizing hours they awaited the signal as the familiar rose tint in the east displayed its first hue of the coming dawn. Suddenly, one soldado in the second column could restrain himself no longer and around 5:00 AM cried out, "Viva Santa Anna! Viva la Republica! Viva Mexico!" His comrades joined in the shouting. With stress already thick at the command post, the orders came quickly and the agreed upon assault signal of rockets were fired, indicating to the columns still silent, that the attack was to commence. A bugle call brought the anxious soldados to attention, while another shrill blast beckoned them to charge. Santa Anna ordered the massed bands to play the frightful notes of the deguello as a reminder to both Mexican soldado and Texian defender that "no quarter" will be given.

As the defenders were forced back to the long barracks, the Mexicans came under "a lively rifle fire from atop the barracks" which caused "painful havoc."

The four Mexican columns encircling the Alamo all surged forward toward the walls. The Texian sentries must have been knifed in their outposts while they slept for they gave no warning. If the rockets or bugles did not wake the defenders the sound of 2,000 footsteps running toward them, getting louder, would have. Inside the Alamo, Travis' adjutant, Captain John Baugh, was the first to raise the alarm. He raced across the compound to the fort's headquarters. "The Mexicans are coming, the Mexicans are coming, Colonel Travis, the Mexicans are coming!" Travis sprang from his cot, grabbed his double-barrel shotgun, and ran to the north wall to meet the threat. "C'mon boys, the Mexicans are upon us and we'll give them Hell!"

In a hellish brutal encounter, soldados fire captured cannon into the long barracks, and then rush in to meet fierce resistance.

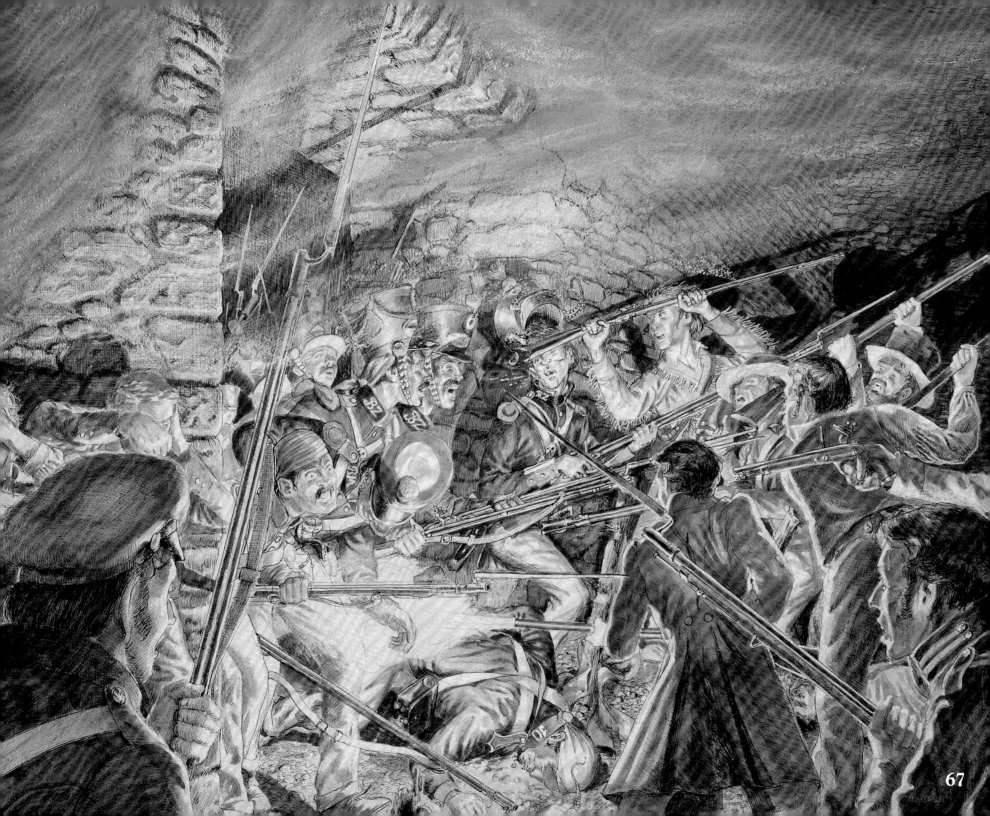

The Texians, aroused from their deep slumber, began to stumble out of the long barracks and other rooms and race to the walls. The defenders had kept their cannons loaded and the gunners fired lethal rounds of canister into the charging Mexican formations. The immediate salvos from the northern batteries cut deadly swaths into the Mexican infantry. A discharge from one cannon inflicted terrible damage on a company of the Toluca Battalion and brought down Colonel Duque. Blistering rifle fire from the Texians caused scores of attackers to drop either dead or wounded. To the east, the combined rifle and cannon fire on Colonel Romero's 300 fusiliers was so devastating the entire column veered north and merged with Colonel Duque's men. The attack was momentarily stunted. All the soldados, except the cazadores battalion to the south, formed a crowded mass beneath the North Wall and the momentum briefly shifted to the Texians' defense. It was then that Santa Anna committed the 400 men of his reserve battalion of Zapadores, his assault engineers, who charged through the chaos at the base of the wall and breached the thinning Texian defences. Amid the hail of lead flying in all directions, perhaps the first Texian casualty was Colonel Travis, who took a musket ball to the head at one of the northern batteries. His slave, Joe, later recalled that the Mexicans had come over the wall that morning "like sheep." Immediately, the momentum had dramatically shifted in favor of the attackers. Once the wall was gained there was no stopping the assault.

Defenders not killed in the compound or the long barracks began to fall back to the church to make a last stand while some elected to break out into the open and take their chances.

To the south, Colonel Morales lead his 120 cazadores toward the lunette, intent on capturing the 2-gun fortification and the main gate. But the Texians had other ideas. The thunderous shower of musket balls and grapeshot from the south wall persuaded Morales to alter his attack plan. The resourceful Mexican commander guided his column around to the southwest corner, placed 2 ladders against the wall and quickly climbed over. The swiftness of this attack caught the defenders by surprise.
A brief but vicious hand-to-hand struggle ensued for control of the southwest corner and the 18-pound cannon. The Texians fought heroically and the Mexicans exhibited great courage in the life or death contest but the defenders were too few and quickly overpowered. The Mexicans were now in control of the southwest corner and pouring into the plaza.

Mexican Officer's Belt Buckle (Bobby McKinney Collection)

Lone Star & Stripes replica flag (Scott McMahon Collection)

70

Amid fierce fighting atop the long barracks, Zapadore Sub-Lieutenant Jose Maria Torres managed to lower the Texian flag and raise the Mexican banner, before being mortally wounded.

71

From atop his gun position at the rear of the church, Captain Dickinson dropped down from the platform ran into the sacristy to embrace his wife, Susanna, and young child for the last time. "Great God, Sue", he cried out, "the Mexicans are inside our walls! All is lost! If they spare you, save my child!" He kissed her farewell and returned to his post. She would never see her husband again.

Turning the cannon on the defenders:

"He (General Amador) had made use of the enemy's own artillery and turned them toward the doors of the small inner rooms in which the rebels had taken cover."

General Vicente Filisola

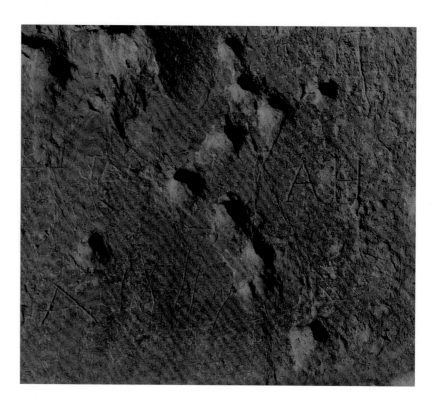

Mexican artillerymen turn cannon against the front entrance of the church and blast the barricade the Texians had placed there.

The entrance to the church is charged by a swarm of soldados who rush in to defeat any lingering resistance hold up inside.

Texian defenders make a final stand atop the battery at the rear of the church. They kept firing at the entering soldados until they were eventually killed.

The Texians began withdrawing to the convento and church buildings as Alamo Plaza filled with soldados. Inside the convento, Texians had dug trenches, and chiselled loopholes into walls so that they could fire with some protection upon their foes. But the plan was fouled when solodados captured the Texians' cannon before the defenders could disable them. The soldados rolled the guns off their ramps over to the ensconced Texians and blew open the doors. Each darkened room and corner became its own separate and personal battleground. Those Texians not killed by the blast were now taken by the bayonet.

As the massed northern columns worked their way towards the convento, the cazadores coming from the south cleared the gate, lunette, and then the campo santo fronting the church. Next to the gate, was a bed-ridden Jim Bowie, who met his end with bayonet thrusts. A number of desperate defenders fled their posts and raced eastward toward the Gonzales Road and home. But before they got to the Acequia Madre to the east, they were lanced, shot, and trod over by the Mexican cavalry that had been placed there. By the time the sun had broken the eastern horizon, the battle was virtually over, but not the killing.

Defenders who broke out into the open were ridden down by Mexican Lancers. Among these Texians was "a very active man" who shot and killed a Lancer named Eugenio.

76

Around 6:30 AM, it was safe enough for Santa Anna and his entourage to enter the Alamo. What awaited him in the battle-scarred fort was more than the horrid scene of hundreds of Mexican and Texian dead and dying strewn throughout the compound. Accounts suggest that as many as 7 defenders outlasted the carnage. When they were presented to His Excellency, he immediately ordered their execution, much to the disgust and protest of several high-ranking officers. David Crockett was said to be one of those who stared death in the eye. They were brutally hacked down by staff officers who had not participated in the battle and desired to prove themselves to their president general. Minutes later the non-combatants were ushered out of the Alamo and taken to the Musquiz house on Main Plaza. Here they were interviewed personally by Santa Anna and given a blanket and 2 dollars. The first messengers of the Alamo's defeat were then coldly dismissed and slowly rode away to the east and into the sad pages of history.

"…there ensued a terrible struggle with blades, and then a pitiful but deserved slaughter of the ungrateful colonists, who threw down their weapons and thought to find safety in escape or by hiding."

Unidentified Mexican soldier

Lancers mopping up the escapee's:

"Sixty-two Texians who sallied from the east side of the fort were received by the lancers and all were killed."

Sargento Manuel Loranca

Two unknown defenders may have escaped the carnage. Overtaken by a refugee family on the road to Nacogdoches, they confirmed the Alamo had fallen.

The grim scene in front of the church was "littered with corpses and scattered limbs." It was here, Mrs. Dickinson later claimed to have witnessed Crockett's body.

That afternoon, the Texians bodies were hauled to the Alameda to be burned. A pyre on each side of the road made the warning very clear as to how Santa Anna's centralist government would deal with "Pirates." Within months, nature worked its way to scatter most of the remains, but the Alamo story would continue to live.

The aftermath (dead and dying)

"Such a dreadful sight. Mexican soldiers with smoke and dirt begrimed faces, haggard eyes and wild, insane expression. The odor was oppressive and sickening and the simply horrible scene nerved us as nothing could."

Eulalia Yorba

"The victory will cost the enemy so dear, that it will be worse for him than a defeat" (William Travis) *The shock and horror reflected on the face of this soldado is perhaps symbolic of that 'victory.'*

On February 25th, 1837, exactly one year after he left the Alamo as a courier, Colonel Juan N. Seguín returned with his cavalry to San Antonio, and performed a funeral of sorts for the fallen Alamo defenders. The few remaining ashes were "carefully collected" from the pyres and placed in a coffin and interred.

Juan Seguín's Funeral Oration for the Alamo Fallen "Companions in Arms! These remains which we have the honour of carrying on our shoulders are those of the valiant heroes who died in the Alamo. Yes, my friends, they preferred to die a thousand times rather than submit themselves to the tyrant's yoke. What a brilliant example! Deserving of being noted in the pages of history. The spirit of liberty appears to be looking out from its elevated throne with its pleasing mind and point to us saying: "There are your brothers, Travis, Bowie, Crockett, and others whose valour places them in the rank of my heroes." Yes soldiers and fellow citizens, these are the worthy beings who, by the twists of fate, during the present campaign delivered their bodies to the ferocity of their enemies; who, barbarously treated as beasts, were bound by their feet and dragged to this spot, where they were reduced to ashes. The venerable remains of our worth companions as witnesses, I invite you to declare to the entire world, "Texas shall be free and independent or we shall perish in glorious combat."

Alamo Church (from The Illustrated Alamo: 1836)

The Alamo "was an example of unselfish heroism"
and should "be sacred to every man in whose heart throbs
one iota of patriotism and respect for the heroic dead."

Adina de Zavala

Epilogue

Remember the Alamo:
The Journey Beyond the Battle Cry

The Alamo story has affected many people in profound ways.
Within one week of that fateful battle, the first messengers arrived at General Sam Houston's camp in Gonzales. The patchy details of the Alamo's fall by Susannah Dickinson was enough to send a panic wave across Texas, resulting in a mass exodus now known as the Runaway Scrape. Six weeks later, Sam Houston's army suddenly changed the course of history, on April 21st, by launching a surprise attack at San Jacinto (near present day Houston). Amid the battle cry, "Remember the Alamo!" Santa Anna's entire advance force was crushed. With the capture of Santa Anna the very next day, Texas Independence was virtually secured. For a brief moment across the new republic and the United States, the name "Alamo" was on everyone's lips...but fame can be fleeting.

The Alamo, it seems, was destined to struggle. Even in its formation it had to fight for its existence. The monks who carved the stone and built the walls, were forced to abandon the mission, leaving it unfinished; never to become the edifice of peace and beauty it was intended to be. In spite of being forsaken by its creators, the Alamo would endure. The adobe brick and limestone mission would continue to offer itself as a sanctuary and shelter to those in need of its quiet rooms or protective walls.
Over the passage of time, the destructive forces of nature, neglect, and indifference began to take its toll. The retreating Mexican army demolished all of the adobe walls and fortifications but left the strong stone buildings. The fortress of freedom had become a total ruin and within time...a forgotten ruin.

"The room(s) have since been demolished, together with the walls which Travis defended, and the barracks... all are gone. The Vandal hand of progress has done its work...While the truck-cart of traffic rumbles over the identical ground that drank in the life blood of those devoted men."

John Southerland, Alamo Courier

In the decades that followed the heroic battle, the town of San Antonio experienced substantial growth in its population, and the Alamo witnessed significant property development on its ever-shrinking borders. Buildings of different shapes and sizes began to spring-up all around the Alamo to the point where the revered old mission was being crowded out and threatened with extinction. Even up until the early 1900's, real estate speculators and developers cast a hungry eye upon the mission property, indifferent to its historic contributions. Not much has changed since those early years. Though some efforts have been made, the Alamo still struggles for its existence, its identity, and the full meaning of it's unique history.

If we are to save and maintain our historic sites, we must remain vigilant. We must raise our level of consciousness and get involved in the preservation process, or watch our unique heritage slowly erode. In today's fast-paced and ever changing world, we need our historic places to remind us of who we are; both as a nation and a people. We thirst for value-based bastions – like the Alamo – so that we may contemplate the heroic deeds of brave and noble men, connect with altruistic ideals, and recall the timeless lessons of Duty – Honor – Country.

About the Authors

Gary L. Foreman

has worked in multiple aspects of the media and film production since 1972, including producing and directing, professional photography, creative & technical writing, historical consulting, talent advisor, and set design. In 1980 he began focusing his talents towards the educational field, including historical documentaries, cultural programming, and historic preservation. In 1998, he founded Native Sun Productions, a multiple award-winning, full-service production company specializing in television, print, museum design and large format EPICArt®. Clients include A&E, History Channel, Discovery, PBS, Colonial Williamsburg, NPS, NBC, Bob Bullock TX State History Museum, US Army, and many more. Major awards include 3 coveted Western Heritage Awards, 4 Western Writers of America, NEMN Bronze Apple, Int'l CINDY Award, and a Primetime EMMY nomination.

Mark H. Lemon

was born in Georgia in 1955 and received a Bachelor of Fine Arts Degree at the University of Georgia. After a career as an officer in the US Navy, and Special Agent for the NCIS, he moved back to Georgia and began work as a private investigator.
As an artist and history enthusiast, he authored The Illustrated Alamo 1836, A Photographic Journey (State House Press 2008). This groundbreaking work features his meticulously crafted architectural model of the Alamo with hand-rendered drawings, setting a new standard in the accurate visual depiction of the Alamo, and garnering him the Reuben F. Potter Award for scholastic excellence in TX history, and the Art & Architecture Award from the Alamo Society. Recent research has revealed that he is related to Alamo defenders, William P. King and Galba Fuqua.

Author

Historical Advisor

Glenn A. Effler
was born in Englewood, New Jersey in 1957.
He enlisted in the U. S. Air Force in 1977 and
was trained as an Aircrew Life Support Specialist.
He taught outdoor survival and emergency
parachuting at the U.S. Air Force Academy
in Colorado Springs, Colorado, until his retirement
in 1997. A lifelong Alamo aficionado and student of
Texas history, he has taken the first step in
fulfilling his dream of writing about the Alamo
and not just reading about it. He is a member
of the Alamo Society and the Alamo Battlefield As-
sociation and devotes his spare time working
on the Alamo Plaza Restoration Project.
Glenn currently resides in Denver, Colorado.

COL (R) Alan C. Huffines
is an 8th generation Texan, and decorated Persian
Gulf War veteran. He holds both a B.A. in history
from Midwestern State University, Wichita Falls,
TX, and a M.A. in history from Norwich University,
Montpelier, VT. He is a member of Western Writers
of America and the Company of Military Historians.
He has authored several books, Killed by the Indians
1871 (TX Wesleyan Univ. Press 2010), The Texas
War of Independence 1835-36 (Osprey Publishing
2005), A Pilgrim Shadow (Eakin Press 2001), and
Blood of Noble Men: The Alamo Siege & Battle
(Eakin Press 1999). He has also served as a military
and historical advisor for television and feature films,
the most recent being The Alamo (Touchstone
2004).

Acknowledgements

FINAL THOUGHTS FROM THE AUTHORS

"I know I speak for our team when I say this work rides on the shoulders of so many passionate Alamo scholars and artists who have come before us. And whether it's that scholar or common traveler, it is our profound desire, with each page that is absorbed and turned to the next that this evolving story can be inspiring, and intimately shared with generations to come. It is, after all, a timeless story that transcends our contrived and self-imposed differences, and beckons us to remember this Sacred Ground. We know it today as Alamo Plaza."
Gary L. Foreman

"The art of the Alamo has for too long been inexcusably rooted in sentimentality and pop-culture. For generations, some of the most dramatic, tragic and exciting events associated with it have gone visually undocumented. Yet, for the serious historic artist who cares to dig deeper, the Alamo story is an untapped resource rife with source material. In this book, I have attempted to explore previously uncharted territory in order to forge a new artistic vision of that tragic and heroic chapter in Texas' history. It is my sincere wish that these illustrations will help bring the viewer a bit closer to what actually happened during those fateful 13 days." Mark Lemon

"13 The Alamo Book of Days is the achievement of a very talented team and I'm proud to have contributed in the formation of its stirring pages. As a young boy, the tale of the Alamo has both fascinated and inspired me. It still does today. It's been a joy and a privilege to write the story of this enduring symbol of freedom and of the men who gave their last full measure. I'd like to express my undying gratitude to Gary Foreman and Mark Lemon for their beautiful imagery and giving the story "life." And a special thanks to COL (R) Alan C. Huffines, whose impeccable credentials made him the ideal choice as historical consultant. It is my hope this book will take you on a historical journey which will propel you ever forward." Glenn Effler

This book would not have been possible without the generous assistance of many friends, experts, collectors, and dedicated historians. First, we wish to thank Gary L. Foreman for his vision (and persistence) in making this book a reality. Gary's stunning photography brings the intimate and authentic details of history to life. We also wish to thank Mark Lemon for his amazing illustrations that capture moments in time that no one has seen before. Mark is a master with light, through his attention to color, shading and detail that makes you feel like you are there. An additional thank you to both Mark and Gary for allowing us to use a few realistic photographs from Mark's amazing book, The Illustrated Alamo: 1836 (State House Press), and to Jim Boddie for some exciting new maps. We want to thank Glenn Effler for his wonderful writing that is both historically and emotionally stirring. Glenn has presented both the known and little-known facts surrounding this legendary event with insightfulness and depth. We also want to thank Alan C. Huffines for laying the foundation of this story by contributing his vast historical knowledge of this unique time and place, as well as loaning us his props and wardrobe from the 2004 Alamo movie. This book would not have come together without the combined talents of Lynn Beda, Susan Gamble, Michael Gamble Jr., and Bill Hamilton; graphic design artists, extraordinaire. We wish to thank the following individuals for allowing us to photograph their private collections: Joe Musso, Joe Swann, Bobby McKinney, and Johnnie Bubenik. Thank you to Steve Abolt of Allegheny Arsenal, for his meticulous attention to detail in creating much of the historically authentic clothing used on many of our reenactor models. Steve is 'the' master tailor, bringing both military and civilian clothing styles back that haven't been seen since 1836.

Bringing our historical characters to life would not have been possible without the genuine enthusiasm and patience of our reenactor/models: Bill & Jan Sheets, Thad & Laura Stern, Alfred Cruz, Louie Lopez, Mark Hayden, Alan Selge, Fernando Quintero, Pedro Bernal, Jasmine Quintana, Mark Wedow, Ryan Wedow, Martin Vasquez, Adam Dominguez, Charles Lara, Robert Rendon, Phillip De La Pena, Brad Stansbury, Jerry Layton, Mark Baker, Jay Eben, Rusty Cottrel, Dave Clifton, Sylvia Carrier, Harold Raleigh, Darbin Ousley, Don Dickerson, Travis Kelly, Levi Salazar, Scott McMahon, John Destatte, John Carson, Bill Nowak, Rayford Sewell, Carey Headley, Paul Hartmann, and the 2nd KY Militia.

We'd like to thank our media colleagues, Kreg Lauterbach and Andy Pickard for filming this adventure "on the road".

And finally, having a second 'home' in San Antonio would not be possible without our good friend Ben LaRosa. Ben has provided shelter, occasional shuttling around town, lively discussions, and much laughter.